The Ten Commandments of Progressive Christianity

MICHAEL J. KRUGER

CruciformPress

CruciformPress.com | info@CruciformPress.com

ENDORSEMENTS

"It's amazing just how many of these new 'Ten Commandments' are taken for granted in our culture and also roll easily off the tongue in Christian circles. As a highly gifted surgeon, Michael Kruger refuses to offer a light diagnosis or superficial cures. This is a timely and convicting analysis that we all need to hear."

Michael Horton, Westminster Seminary California

"Don't let the brevity of this book fool you. Mike Kruger has written a trenchant critique of the intellectual bankruptcy and theological deviancy of progressive Christianity. Churches, pastors, students, youth groups, Christian schools, and Christian colleges would do well to appropriate the wisdom in this short but devastating little book."

Kevin DeYoung, Senior Pastor, Christ Covenant Church (Matthews, NC); Assistant Professor of Systematic Theology, Reformed Theological Seminary, Charlotte

"I recognize these Ten Commandments of Progressive Christianity from growing up in the Protestant mainline and from many churches in my community today. There's nothing new in their message, even as such churches portray themselves as our future. Michael Kruger helps us see the internal inconsistencies of their teaching as they decry certainty with, well, certainty. We must be equipped to see why such attempts to revise Christianity will never turn the world upside down, as did the apostles with the good news that Jesus Christ is Lord."

Collin Hansen, editorial director, The Gospel Coalition; author of *Blind Spots: Becoming a Courageous, Compassionate, and Commissioned Church*

Table of Contents

INTRODUCTION 5

1 Jesus Is a Model for Living More Than an
Object for Worship................................. 7

2 Affirming People's Potential Is More
Important Than Reminding Them of Their
Brokenness 13

3 The Work of Reconciliation Should Be
Valued over Making Judgments................. 17

4 Gracious Behavior Is More Important Than
Right Belief... 21

5 Inviting Questions Is More Valuable Than
Supplying Answers 25

6 Encouraging the Personal Search Is More
Important Than Group Uniformity 29

7 Meeting Actual Needs Is More Important
Than Maintaining Institutions.................. 35

8 Peacemaking Is More Important Than Power .. 39

9 We Should Care More about Love and Less
about Sex 45

10 Life in This World Is More Important Than
the Afterlife 51

AUTHOR

Michael J. Kruger is the President and the Samuel C. Patterson Professor of New Testament and Early Christianity at Reformed Theological Seminary in Charlotte, NC. He is ordained in the Presbyterian Church in America.

 *We all know the feeling: every week, every month, every year it just seems that life keeps moving faster and faster. So we've taken our trademark length—books of about 100 pages—and added a set of resources that will make for even a quicker read. Cruciform Quick: a new line of booklets in the range of 40 to 60 pages each.*

THE TEN COMMANDMENTS OF PROGRESSIVE CHRISTIANITY

Print / PDF ISBN: 978-1-949253-21-4
Mobipocket ISBN: 978-1-949253-22-1
ePub ISBN: 978-1-949253-23-8

A Master Class in Half-Truths

In 1923, J. Gresham Machen, then a professor at Princeton Seminary, wrote his classic text, *Christianity and Liberalism*.[1] The book was a response to the rise of liberalism in the mainline denominations of his own day. Machen argued that the liberal understanding of Christianity was, in fact, not just a variant version of the faith, nor did it represent simply a different denominational perspective, but was an entirely different religion. Put simply, liberal Christianity is not Christianity.

What is remarkable about Machen's book is how prescient it was. His description of liberal Christianity—a moralistic, therapeutic version of the faith that values questions over answers and being "good" over being "right"—is still around today in basically the same form. For this reason alone the book should be required reading, certainly for all seminary students, pastors, and Christian leaders.

Although its modern advocates present liberal Christianity as something new and revolutionary, it is nothing of the sort. It may have new names (e.g., "emerging" or "progressive" Christianity), but it is simply a rehash of the same well-worn system that has been around for generations.

The abiding presence of liberal Christianity struck me not long ago when I came across a daily devotional from Richard Rohr that listed ten principles he thinks modern Christianity needs to embody. These ten principles are actually drawn from Philip Gulley's book, *If the Church Were Christian: Rediscovering the Values of Jesus*.[2]

In this devotional series, ironically titled "Returning to Essentials,"[3] Rohr sets forth the ten principles as a kind of confessional statement of modern liberalism (while at the same time pretending to deplore confessional statements). They are, in effect, a Ten Commandments for progressive Christianity.

Indeed, these ten sound like they were gathered not so much on the mountaintop as in the university classroom. They are less about God revealing his desires and more about man expressing his own—less Moses, more Oprah.

But take note: each of these commandments is partially true. Indeed, that is what makes this list, and progressive Christianity as a whole, so challenging. It is a master class in half-truths that sound appealing on the surface until you dig down deeper and really explore their foundations and implications. Benjamin Franklin was right when he quipped, "Half the truth is often a great lie."

Over the next ten chapters we will diagnose and critique each of these tenets, offering a biblical and theological response to each, and dipping occasionally into Machen's classic volume. If the church is going to hold fast to "the faith that was once for all delivered to the saints" (Jude 3), then we must be able to distinguish the true faith from those things that masquerade as the true faith.

My hope and prayer is that this brief volume will make that vital task just a little bit easier.

CHAPTER 1

Jesus Is a Model for Living More Than an Object for Worship

Let's jump right into the first commandment: *Jesus is a model for living more than an object of worship.*

In many ways, this is a fitting first commandment for progressive Christianity. When given the choice between worshiping Jesus (which requires that he is divine) and merely looking at Jesus as a good moral guide, liberals have always favored the latter.

Of course, one might object that this first commandment isn't really rejecting the divinity of Jesus because of the phrase *more than.* Could it be that progressive Christianity affirms the divinity of Jesus but just puts the priority on his moral example?

Not according to Gulley's book. Plainly and unabashedly, Gulley rejects the virgin birth, the sinlessness of Jesus, and the miracles of Jesus as myths designed to elevate Jesus to a "divine status." Indeed, Gulley insists that "the church's worship of Jesus is something he would not have favored."[4]

So it's clear that the progressives are not merely putting the priority on Jesus as a moral example. Rather they are directly rejecting the divine status of Jesus. And such a move is nothing new. In Machen's day, this is also how liberal Christianity operated:

> Liberalism regards Him as an Example and a Guide; Christianity as a Saviour: liberalism makes Him an example for faith; Christianity, the object of faith.[5]

But we must dive deeper into this issue. Does Christianity work if Jesus is simply a moral example? Several problems arise here.

JESUS CLAIMED TO BE MORE THAN A MORAL EXAMPLE

We can begin by acknowledging that Jesus was, of course, a moral example for his followers. Indeed, he often called his followers to do what he has done (e.g., John 13:15).

But is Jesus *merely* a moral example? Or to put it differently, do the Gospels present Jesus as just a wise sage—a Gandhi-like figure offering tips for practical living?

An honest reading of the Gospels shows the answer to this is a resounding *no*. Indeed, throughout these texts, Jesus is presented as not merely a good teacher but as the divine Lord of heaven and earth. Aside from the obvious Johannine passages that show this (e.g., John 1:1; 1:18; 8:58; 10:30), scholars have argued that Jesus's divinity is also evident in the Synoptic Gospels of Matthew, Mark, and Luke.

As just one example, Michael Bird's recent book, *Jesus the Eternal Son*,[6] has argued that even Mark—often thought to be the Gospel which presents the most "human" Jesus—offers a decidedly high Christology. Jesus is the "Lord," Yahweh visiting his people, the one who forgives sins, the ruler of the wind and the waves, and the judge of all the universe. This reality led C.S. Lewis to offer his well-known quote on Jesus as "just" a good moral teacher:

> I am trying here to prevent anyone saying the really foolish thing that people often say about him: I'm

ready to accept Jesus as a great moral teacher, but I don't accept his claim to be God. That is the one thing we must not say. A man who was merely a man and said the sort of things Jesus said would not be a great moral teacher. He would either be a lunatic—on the level with the man who says he is a poached egg—or else he would be the Devil of Hell. You must make your choice.[7]

JESUS' FOLLOWERS WORSHIPED HIM AS LORD

While the first commandment of progressive Christianity seems quite hesitant about worshiping Jesus, that is not how the earliest Christians felt. Indeed, because Jesus was viewed as their Lord, they unreservedly devoted themselves to worshiping him.

And here's the kicker: the earliest Christians did this while also being fully committed to monotheism. Even as Jews, they worshiped Jesus precisely because they believed he was the one true God of Israel.

We should also note that Jesus never rejected this worship. Nor did he seem sheepish, uncomfortable, or hesitant about it. He welcomed it without reservation. A few examples:

- The Magi worship Jesus (Matthew 2:11).
- The disciples worship Jesus on the boat (Matthew 14:33).
- The disciples worship Jesus after his resurrection (Matthew 28:9; Luke 24:52).
- The man born blind worships Jesus (John 9:38).
- Every knee will bow in worship of the Lord Jesus (Philippians 2:10).
- The angels worship Jesus (Hebrews 1:6).

- Virtually the entire book of Revelation is about the worship of Jesus.

And this quick sampling does not even consider the numerous doxological declarations offered to Jesus, nor does it consider worship practices of the earliest Christians showing the type of devotion to Christ that is reserved for God alone.[8]

JESUS' MORAL EXAMPLE IS BINDING ONLY IF HE IS LORD

While liberal Christians make much of Jesus' moral example, what is so oddly missing in their system is why anyone should care. After all, if Jesus is just an ordinary man, why would we think his particular moral code is any better than anyone else's? Why should we think his moral code matters at all?

Indeed, isn't it the progressive Christian system that is always pushing back against people who make absolute moral claims? Morality is relative, we are told. Morality is ever-changing and culturally conditioned. There is no one true morality; don't push *your* morality on me.

So why should Jesus get a pass? Why do such criticisms not apply to him, if he is just another human being like us?

I suppose one could argue that Jesus has moral authority not because he is divine, but because he is a prophet from God. But how does one *know* he is a prophet from God? Scripture is the only way we know enough about Jesus to draw such a conclusion.

This, of course, just raises the question of what progressives think about Scripture. Many progressives don't take Scripture as reliable and plainly reject its inspiration. And if Scripture is unreliable and uninspired, how do they know Jesus is a prophet?

Other progressives might want to claim that they accept the inspiration of Scripture. But if they do that, why don't they accept the plain teaching of Scripture that Jesus is not just a prophet? Why don't they accept the passages above that show Jesus as the all-deserving object of worship?

Either way, the progressive Jesus-is-just-a-good-moral-teacher approach simply doesn't work.

On top of all of this, one might understandably be confused by the progressive appeal to Jesus as a guide for morality when many progressives won't, in fact, *follow* Jesus' moral teaching! For example, are progressives willing to stand by Jesus' plain teaching that marriage is between a man and a woman (e.g., Matthew 19:5–6)? Or that he is the only way of salvation (John 14:6)?

If not, then why the eagerness to appeal to him as a moral teacher?

CHRISTIANITY IS NOT ABOUT MORALISM

Here is where we come to the most foundational problem with this first tenet. By removing the person of Jesus from the equation as an object of worship, it essentially makes Christianity a religion of moralism. What matters most, we are told, is not doctrine or theology, but behavior. Deeds over creeds.

But this absolutely contrary to historic Christianity, which is a religion of grace, not a religion of merit. It's not primarily about what *we* do, but what God has done in Christ. Or, in the words of John: "In this is love, not that we have loved God but that he loved us and sent his Son to be the propitiation for our sins" (1 John 4:10). Machen himself captured it well:

> Here is found the most fundamental difference between liberalism and Christianity—liberalism is

altogether in the imperative mood, while Christianity begins with a triumphant indicative; liberalism appeals to man's will, while Christianity announces, first, a gracious act of God.[9]

WHAT GOD HAS JOINED TOGETHER

This first commandment of progressive Christianity precisely reflects what has been happening in the Western world for more than a century. It represents yet another vain attempt to preserve Jesus' morality while jettisoning his divine identity.

In the end, this simply doesn't work. Jesus' moral teaching only works when we retain his identity as Lord. The two should never and can never be split apart.

"What therefore God has joined together, let not man separate" (Matthew 19:6).

Affirming People's Potential Is More Important Than Reminding Them of Their Brokenness

There are few issues that divide progressive Christianity from historic Christianity more than the issue of sin. Indeed, it is the loss, downplaying, ignoring, or sometimes even the outright rejection of sin that fundamentally defines progressive Christianity. Generations ago, Machen made this same observation: "At the very root of the modern liberal movement is the loss of the consciousness of sin."[10]

We come then to the second commandment of progressive Christianity: *Affirming people's potential is more important than reminding them of their brokenness.*

The core issue in this second tenet is the issue of sin.[11] Are people sinners? If so, how big of a deal is it? More than that, how important is it that people *know* they are sinners? Should we tell them? And how we do balance people's sinfulness with their potential as God's image-bearers?

BALANCING SIN AND HUMAN POTENTIAL

Of course, we should acknowledge from the outset that this second tenet is partially true. The Christian message is not *only* about our sin and our brokenness. "You are a sinner" is not all that can or should be said. Christ saves us from our sin, yes, but then he begins a renewing work inside each believer. And that renewing work begins to restore the beauty of God's image within us.

In that sense, we can truly say that people have potential. And that potential should be affirmed and celebrated. But we cannot forget that it is potential wrought only by the saving grace of God and the death of Christ, which conquered our sin. Apart from that, any affirmation of human potential quickly devolves into a version of humanistic moralism.

Put differently, we must affirm *both* our deep depravity and the amazing potential we have as God's image-bearers. The two belong together.

But this is precisely the problem with the progressive message. They are eager to accept the latter, but hesitant about the former. Again, they have separated what the Bible joins.

REJECTING THE BIBLE'S TEACHING ON SIN

Now one might object that not all progressives deny the sinfulness of humanity. Some progressives, it could be argued, are quite willing to affirm both of these truths.

But if we return to Gulley's book—the basis of Rohr's list—we quickly discover that Gulley himself does not affirm both truths. In fact, he is quite adamant that the historical Christian teaching about sin is fundamentally mistaken. Consider the following:

Gulley argues that churches that regularly teach that people are sinners are guilty of "spiritual abuse" and "mistreatment" of their people. [12]

Gulley states plainly, "I had grown up in a tradition that emphasized sin and the need for salvation, hadn't found it helpful, and had resolved to leave it behind." [13]

Gulley denies original sin on the grounds that Adam and Eve were not real people; the stories are just religious "myths." Moreover, the creation stories cannot be trusted anyway because they're contradictory and inconsistent. [14]

Gulley argues that we should stop "viewing ourselves as wretched sinners, deserving of damnation." He even laments hymns like "Amazing Grace" that speak of God saving sinners. [15]

REJECTING THE SAVING WORK OF CHRIST

Rejecting the biblical teaching on sin is one thing. But lurking behind it is the rejection of an even more fundamental Christian truth, namely that the purpose of Jesus' death was to save us from our sins.

If one rejects the doctrine of sin and downplays its seriousness, one must find a different reason for why Christ died. For progressives (at least those like Gulley), Jesus couldn't be dying on the cross to pay for sins because that would imply sin is a big deal. No, Christ must be dying for some *other* reason. Thus we come to another major tenet of progressive Christianity: the rejection of the substitutionary atonement.

Gulley states:

> The church has typically understood salvation as being rescued from sin and going to heaven when we die. But what if we believed salvation was our life-long journey toward maturity, love, and wholeness? Were that the case, *Jesus would not be the one who saves humanity by his sacrifice of blood*, but the one who exemplifies this maturity, love and wholeness, the one to whom Christians can look and say…'we can be like him!'"[16]

So we see that this version of progressive Christianity does not reject only the doctrine of sin. It rejects the saving work of Christ on the cross. Once again, Christianity is reduced to mere moralism.

PROGRESSIVE CHRISTIANITY (OR AT LEAST THIS VERSION) IS NOT CHRISTIANITY

After one has jettisoned the doctrine of original sin, rejected the idea that we are therefore sinners in need of salvation, and denied that Jesus died on the cross for sins, what is left of historical, biblical Christianity? Not much. Indeed, Machen would argue that we are left with something that is not Christianity. It is something else altogether.

We would do better to trust the simple and clear message of the apostle Paul: "The saying is trustworthy and deserving of full acceptance, that Christ Jesus came into the world to save sinners" (1 Timothy 1:15).

CHAPTER 3

The Work of Reconciliation Should Be Valued over Making Judgments

One of the hallmarks of progressive Christianity is that it focuses less on the way humans relate to God and more on how humans relate to humans. This concern is evident in the third commandment: *The work of reconciliation should be valued over making judgments.*

Gulley is concerned here with broken or estranged human relationships. The church should do more to repair and restore these relationships but, in his view, is too busy condemning people's behavior. Christians need to stop judging and start helping.

Now, we can begin by acknowledging that the goal here is commendable. Bringing reconciliation to broken human relationships is a fundamental biblical value. The Bible has much to say on topics like forgiving one another (Luke 17:4), being reconciled to one another (Matthew 5:24; Acts 7:26), husbands and wives reconciling (1 Corinthians 7:11), and the removal of hostility between groups (Ephesians 2:16). Indeed, Gulley is correct that reconciliation between humans is an important aspect of Christianity.

The problem, though, is *how* Gulley thinks that reconciliation is best achieved. And it is here that he takes a biblical value and puts a decidedly progressive/liberal spin on it. Reconciliation between humans is best achieved, he argues, when the church is less concerned with "making judgments." If only the church would get rid of its "culture of judgment," stop offering "judgment and blame," and "surrender its fondness for black-and-white, either-or thinking," then it could better help people reconcile with one another.[17]

Now, again, it depends on what one means by such statements. If the concern here is merely with a church's overall *tone* or *attitude,* then point made. Churches need to be careful, even in the midst of dealing with sin, to be gracious, patient, and charitable. But if these statements mean that the church should not be in the business of calling out people's behavior as sinful or wrong, then that is something very different.

Indeed, that sort of approach has several significant problems.

TO SAY WE CAN NEVER DECLARE A BEHAVIOR TO BE WRONG IS PROFOUNDLY UNBIBLICAL

The Scriptures are packed with examples of God's people calling out certain behaviors as wrong. Jesus did this. Paul did this. And even we are called to do this: "If your brother sins against you, go and tell him his fault" (Matthew 18:15).

At this point a person might object, "But who am I to tell someone they are wrong? I am a sinner too." Yes, and that's an essential perspective to maintain. But the Bible never requires a person to be sinless before they speak out against sin. Personal perfection is not a prerequisite to standing up for what is right. Otherwise no one would ever be able to condemn sin—including (as we'll see in a moment) those who want to condemn those who judge!

The proper basis for calling something sinful is not personal perfection, but simply whether *God* regards it as sinful.

TO SAY WE CAN NEVER DECLARE A BEHAVIOR TO BE WRONG IS ULTIMATELY SELF-DEFEATING

The great irony for those who say we shouldn't judge is that they themselves are judging. They are declaring a behavior to be "wrong" (in this case, the behavior of judging), while at the same time insisting that we shouldn't declare that behaviors are wrong! Thus, this approach proves to be profoundly inconsistent. It is the rhetorical equivalent of sawing off the branch you're sitting on.

In this way, progressive Christianity is very much the product of today's cultural climate. We live in a world that insists, more than ever, that we should not judge. But we also live in a world that is one of the most angry and judgmental in generations. Like never before, people feel free to express, often quite vigorously, their moral outrage at just about any grievance (as those active on social media can attest). Yet they remain seemingly unaware of how this behavior fails to square with their professed commitment to not judging.

TO SAY WE CAN NEVER DECLARE A BEHAVIOR TO BE WRONG IS INEVITABLY SELECTIVE

One curiosity of the progressive insistence that we should not be people who "judge" is that it is selectively applied. When it comes to sexual ethics, for example, we are told we should not judge others. Everyone should be allowed to express themselves as they wish. But when it comes to racism, environmentalism, abuse, or other similar issues, then apparently judging the behavior of others is allowable. Indeed, it is required!

TO SAY WE CAN NEVER DECLARE A BEHAVIOR TO BE WRONG UNDERCUTS THE PROCESS OF RECONCILIATION

The fundamental problem with the progressive approach to judging is that it undercuts the very goal it is trying to achieve, namely human reconciliation. Such reconciliation can only happen when wrongs are acknowledged, owned, and repented of. And in order for that to happen, judgments must be made about people's behavior. And that behavior must *really* be wrong—not just wrong in someone's *opinion*. Otherwise, reconciliation is a mirage.

We can and do affirm that human reconciliation is an important biblical value. And we can and do affirm that churches should not have a judgmental *tone* or *attitude*—they should always operate with grace, patience, and a spirit of love. But none of this requires us to abandon God's clear teaching that some things ought to be declared right and other things declared wrong.

That is the proper form of judging. And it is not something to avoid, but something we are called to do. As the prophet Isaiah said, "Woe to those who call evil good and good evil" (Isaiah 5:20).

CHAPTER 4

Gracious Behavior Is More Important Than Right Belief

As we've seen, progressive Christianity is largely defined by its focus on morality and its downplaying of doctrine. What truly matters, we are told, is not what we believe but how we behave. This brings us to the fourth commandment: *Gracious behavior is more important than right belief.*

Upon a first reading, there is room here for some common ground. We certainly would agree that gracious behavior should characterize the church (though there may be disagreement about what exactly that entails). At a minimum, we could say that the church (and Christians) should be patient, gentle, kind, and loving to everyone—even those who have different theological convictions.

Yet there are also a number of concerns that arise from the way this commandment is phrased, and with the way Gulley fleshes out the specifics.

IS THE PURSUIT OF GOOD THEOLOGY THE PROBLEM?

The prioritization of behavior over theology sells well to our modern world because the general population already has the idea that people who care about theology are divisive, narrow, dogmatic, and even mean. What matters instead, we are told, is that we simply be kind to people.

Gulley drives home the stereotype by comparing people who care about theology with the Pharisees. The problem with the Pharisees, argues Gulley, is their "fixation on orthodoxy" and their "misguided quest for theological purity."[18] Translation: if you care about orthodoxy you are probably just another Pharisee.

Leaving aside the ungracious (!) nature of this comparison, we can simply observe how historically inaccurate it is. Jesus never said the problem with the Pharisees is that they are too concerned with orthodoxy. The problem with the Pharisees was legalism (putting man-made laws ahead of God's) and hypocrisy (saying one thing and doing another). And the two often went together. It wasn't that they cared too much about good theology, but that they cared too little! Their theology was a mess. It glorified man, twisted God's own priorities, and selectively followed God's law.

This raises an important point. Teaching people good theology is not the problem, but the solution. Teaching people good theology is a vital, essential way of caring for them. Rather than viewing theology as something that harms and oppresses people, we should be reminded that good theology actually comforts and liberates people. The Pharisees harmed people precisely by teaching them (and modeling for them) *bad* theology.

IS BEHAVIOR MORE IMPORTANT THAN THEOLOGY?

Another issue with this fourth commandment is the dichotomy it creates between behavior and doctrine. The former is simply more important than the latter, we are told.

But the problem here is that the two cannot be so easily divided. Indeed, any declaration about right or wrong behavior is a *theological* declaration! One cannot determine godly behavior in the absence of sound theological categories and concepts, for behavior is only "right" if it fits with God's law and God's character.

There is a rich irony here. The statement, "Gracious behavior is more important than right belief" is itself a statement about what we should believe! Apparently "right belief" matters after all.

DO WE GET MORE "GRACE" BY PRIORITIZING BEHAVIOR?

Gulley's push to prioritize behavior over doctrine is driven by a simple conviction, namely that it leads people to be more *gracious*. He claims, "Jesus knew ungracious behavior often had its roots in a misguided quest for theological purity." [19] In other words, good theology doesn't tend to produce gracious behavior. Instead, argues Gulley, we get *more* gracious behavior from people by focusing more on, well, their behavior.

It is here that Gulley has come full circle and returned to the first of his progressive commandments, namely that Christianity is more about morality than about worshiping Jesus. Simply put, Gulley's basic argument is that gracious behavior flows most readily from moralism. Of course, the sad reality is that it was actually the Pharisees, not Jesus, who were committed to moralism. And their moralism did not, in any way, make them more gracious.

Again, there's an irony here. While on the one hand Gulley critiques the ungracious nature of the Pharisees, on the other hand he advocates the Pharisees' own moralistic methodology. This is universally what happens when doctrine and theology are disparaged. All you're left with is a religion of being "nice" to other people.

If we really want to become people who are more gracious, the answer is not to focus on our behavior and "try harder." Instead, the answer is to focus on Jesus Christ, the Son of God, who gave his life to pay the debt of our sins and empowers us by the Spirit to live a new life. It is then that we can really love others selflessly.

J. Gresham Machen once more sums it up well:

> The strange thing about Christianity was that it adopted an entirely different method [for how people change]. It transformed the lives of men not by appealing to the human will, but by telling a story; not by exhortation, but by the narration of an event... The lives of men are transformed by a piece of news.[20]

The Christian approach requires that we think theologically.

In the end, it's clear that right behavior is not more important than right theology. *Both* are important. As Paul reminds us, "Keep a close watch on yourself and on the teaching" (1 Timothy 4:16).

CHAPTER 5

Inviting Questions Is More Valuable Than Supplying Answers

Perhaps no commandment in the series better captures the ethos of progressive Christianity than the fifth: *Inviting questions is more valuable than supplying answers.*

It's an effective strategy. Position yourself as humble and inquisitive, merely on a journey of discovery. Then position the other side as less-than-humble dispensers of rigid dogma. You're just a well-meaning seeker; they're mean, entrenched know-it-alls. Brilliant. Indeed, this is Gulley's very complaint about the church. He argues that it has been "committed to propaganda" and "towing the party line" instead of engaged in a "vigorous exploration of the truth."[21]

Okay, so what shall we make of this fifth "commandment"? A few thoughts.

A CARICATURE OF CHRISTIANITY

We begin by noting, once more, that there is an element of truth here. The expressions of Christianity found in the United States alone are numerous and varied, and many people are familiar with churches in which quick and rather unsatisfying answers to honest questions about the faith are in ready supply. In these contexts, faith questions are discouraged. Should they arise, the expectation is that you will accept the answer you've been given; serious intellectual engagement is not an option.

If the progressive commandment above is designed merely to correct this kind of approach to Christianity, then point taken. Such a correction is needed. But it would be a caricature to portray Christians (or Christianity) *as a whole* as anti-intellectual propaganda-dispensers. Indeed, most Christians have pressed very hard on the Bible and asked it the toughest of questions—intellectual, historical, and personal. And they have found that it has provided solid and compelling answers. Why should this be a cause for ridicule?

WHICH POSITION IS INTELLECTUALLY IRRESPONSIBLE?

I suspect that part of the issue in play here is that progressives think it is intellectually irresponsible to make the kind of truth-claims that Christians have historically made. It sounds arrogant. Even cocksure. How could anyone know such a thing? The better course of action, they argue, is to say, "I don't know."

While this approach gives off an air of humility, there are significant problems with it. For one, "I don't know" is only the right answer if in fact there is no epistemological basis by which a person could know something. But what if a person does, in fact, have a basis for knowing? If he does, then saying "I don't know" would be irresponsible.

In other words, "I don't know" is not always the right answer. Sometimes it's the wrong answer.

Imagine you recently took a class on the Civil War. If a friend then asks, "Did Abraham Lincoln sign the Emancipation Proclamation?" and you answer "Yes," you could hardly be chided as an arrogant know-it-all. Indeed, if you had answered "I don't know" out of some mistaken notion of intellectual humility then you ought to be chided for rejecting a clear historical truth.

Of course, progressives will argue this is a false comparison because we *know* Lincoln signed the Emancipation Proclamation but we don't know that, say, Jesus was raised from the dead. But that is the very thing in dispute! If the Bible is, in fact, the inspired word of God, then arguably we can be *more* certain about the resurrection than about Abraham Lincoln.

The only way the progressive argument works is if one already "knows" the Bible is not the word of God and therefore can declare all its truth-claims to be dubious. But how does the progressive know this? Isn't it off-limits, from the progressive view, to claim absolute knowledge about such things?

To put it another way, in order for the progressive position to be intellectually defensible, one would have to *know* that you *can't know* whether the resurrection actually happened or not. But that would require a high level of intellectual certainty—something the progressive claims one cannot have.

SMUGGLING CERTAINTY THROUGH THE BACK DOOR

This leads to a real problem with the progressive position, namely that it is inconsistent.

Progressive Christianity laments the dogmatism and certainty of biblical Christianity. All would be much better, Gulley argues, if everyone would just admit their uncertainty. Yet he is quite certain about *his* views—so much so that he is quick to condemn other positions. In one instance he describes another person's perspective on conversion as a "childish point of view" from someone clearly "stuck" in a bad theological position.

Here, as in many other instances, Gulley simply smuggles his certainty through the back door. And he is far from alone in this. Progressives are quick to condemn all sorts of behavior they see in the world around them, while insisting that Bible-believing Christians are wrong when *they* do so. For example, consider the debate over same-sex marriage. Notice that we hear very few progressives say things like, "Well, we just don't know the answer here. We can't be certain what to think about it." No, instead we get absolutism. We get certainty. We get dogmatism.

Thus, one gets the impression that the real issue is not certainty at all. It is *what* one is certain about. Progressives have simply swapped one set of certain beliefs for another.

We all have things we are certain about. Things we believe to be true and real. The key question involves the *basis* for our certainty. Christians base their certainty on God's word.

Scripture may be mocked by the world, but it is the place where Jesus himself stood. He declared to his Father, "Your word is truth" (John 17:17).

CHAPTER 6

Encouraging the Personal Search Is More Important Than Group Uniformity

Does Christianity stifle free thinking? Is the church just interested in protecting its own authority?

In his sixth chapter, Gulley answers both questions in the affirmative. He laments the fact that Christians are so concerned about protecting the church from aberrant views that they stifle free thinking and even kick out people who don't conform. This brings us to the sixth progressive commandment: *Encouraging the personal search is more important than group uniformity.*

To make his point, Gulley tells stories about people he knows who were "disfellowshipped" or "shunned" by their churches for certain behaviors or beliefs. They were just trying to think for themselves, but the church was more interested in "group uniformity." Jesus would never have wanted the church to do such things, we are told. Instead, argues Gulley, Jesus was in favor of "spiritual exploration" and "quite comfortable with independent thought and action."[22]

To be sure, Gulley's chapter does make some good points about the way some churches practice church discipline. He's right to be wary of the "shunning" approach of some groups and is certainly correct that some churches (as we noted earlier) are unwilling to engage graciously with people who ask hard questions. But the overall message of his chapter is far too simplistic. Churches that hold firmly to certain truths are portrayed as mean-spirited and vindictive, and those who question those truths are portrayed as heroically fighting the system for the sake of free thinking. And Jesus, of course, would be on the side of the latter group.

This entire narrative may play well with the progressive wing of Christianity, but I think it has significant problems.

CHRISTIANITY IS NOT JUST ABOUT BEING ON A JOURNEY

Progressives love to portray the Christian religion (and all religion, for that matter) as fundamentally a matter of being on a spiritual "journey." Religion is primarily about "exploring" for ourselves what we think about spiritual matters.

The problem is that hidden within this approach is an enormous (and unspoken) assumption, namely that God has *not* clearly revealed himself. Nor has he clearly revealed a message about salvation. Indeed, the assumption underlying this entire progressive narrative is that religion is about humans finding God, rather than about a God who has revealed himself to humans.

If someone thinks such a thing, you could see why he or she would be irritated with biblical Christianity. According to progressives, religion (by definition!) is always in flux. It's a process of seeking God. How arrogant would it be to claim he's been found! In contrast, biblical Christianity argues that God has clearly revealed a message of salvation in Christ Jesus, and that all people everywhere are called to believe in that good news.

THE CHURCH WELCOMES QUESTIONERS

Gulley fosters the perception that churches as a rule don't like people asking questions, because questions are seen as threatening church authority. Again, while there are certainly some churches like that, I don't think it is true for the evangelical church as a whole.

On the contrary, most churches are quite eager to have people ask questions. Indeed, they want people to inquire about the Christian faith and learn what Christians believe and why they believe it. So it seems the liberal complaint about churches is really something else altogether. It's not so much that churches don't welcome questions (I think most do). The progressive's real complaint is that *the church thinks there are answers to many of those questions*!

Gulley's real objection, therefore, is that Christians think there are clear, knowable answers to life's most important spiritual questions. What he really objects to is the Christian belief in *absolute truth*. That is the sticking point.

And that is why liberals will never be satisfied merely by Christians changing their tone or approach. They will only be satisfied when Christians fully abandon their fundamental truth-claims.[23]

JESUS BELIEVED IN CHURCH DISCIPLINE

As already noted, I think Gulley is correct that certain types of shunning are problematic. But he mistakenly cites 1 Corinthians 5:11 as evidence that the apostle Paul advocates the practice in a broad sense.

What Paul advocates is *church discipline*, that process whereby the leaders of a church lovingly correct wayward members who have engaged in serious disobedience (morally or doctrinally). Like all discipline, it ought to be done gently and for the good of the recipient. And despite Gulley's implication that Jesus would be against such a practice, Jesus affirms it plainly in Matthew 18:15–20. In verse 17, he says, "And if he [the wayward brother] refuses to listen even to the church, let him be to you as a Gentile and a tax collector." In 1 Corinthians 5:11, therefore, Paul affirms the very point Jesus is making here: what some may label as "shunning" is sometimes a good and necessary component of an orderly and redemptive process of church discipline.

Keep in mind that church discipline is exclusively for members of the covenant community. These passages do not forbid Christians from interacting with non-Christians or people who disagree. No, as already indicated, the church welcomes non-Christians who want to come and learn about Jesus.

Church discipline is for professing believers who have lost their way, that they might repent of sinful practices and be restored. It is for maintaining the peace and purity of the church.

MISSING THE MESSAGE

Thus, I believe this sixth progressive commandment suffers from a number of assumptions or misunderstandings. It assumes there's no absolute truth (without proving such a thing), it assumes that the church doesn't welcome questions (when, generally speaking, it does), and it misunderstands the nature and purpose of church discipline (which is for the good of the recipient).

Even more fundamentally, the progressive position misses the core Christian message. Christianity is not about mankind's never-ending "journey" to God, but about God's completed journey to us, to save us from our sins. As John reminds us, "In this is love, not that we have loved God, but that he loved us and sent his Son to be the propitiation for our sins" (1 John 4:10).

CHAPTER 7

Meeting Actual Needs Is More Important Than Maintaining Institutions

In his book, *They Like Jesus but Not the Church*,[24] Dan Kimball highlighted a key shift in younger demographics, namely that they are disillusioned with the institutional church. They profess to follow Christ but are skeptical of organized religious structures. This phenomenon is captured in the seventh commandment of progressive Christianity: *Meeting actual needs is more important than maintaining institutions.*

In his seventh chapter, Gulley laments how "institutional functions (and dysfunctions) trump the church's mission and purpose."[25] And, he argues, most Christians are blind to this reality: "It seems to be a common trait among humans and the institutions we create to ignore our flaws even as those failings cripple our ability to function and grow."[26]

Gulley offers a number of helpful observations in this chapter, but there is also an underlying anti-institutional vibe that ends up divorcing Jesus from his bride, the church.

THE CHURCH IS NOT PERFECT

Gulley is certainly correct that the church is an imperfect

institution. He offers numerous examples of churches that have been stingy, ingrown, and obsessed with self-preservation and the bottom line. In particular, he notes how too many churches are run like businesses, creating a corporate culture that tends to operate like a Fortune 500 company rather than the bride of Christ. Such churches are more concerned about their "stock price" than they are the needs of the people and community around them.

There is a lot to agree with here, and I am sure every reader could add their own stories of weaknesses in the modern church. Filled with sinners and part of a fallen world, every church clearly (and inevitably) has flaws.

THE CHURCH IS STILL THE BRIDE OF CHRIST

Even so, the church remains Christ's glorious and wonderful bride, dearly loved and cleansed by his blood (Ephesians 5:25–27). Though she will not be perfected until Christ's return, she is still rightly regarded as holy—set apart for God.

Unfortunately, Gulley does not share this high view of the church. For him, the church as an institution is relatively dispensable. Why? Because, in his view, it has little to do with Jesus. He argues, "Jesus appeared to give [the church] little thought... neither its genesis nor continuance seemed a priority to him."[27]

Of course, such statements are stunning when read next to what Jesus actually said about the church. Jesus did not view the church as something man would build but something *he* would build. "I will build *my* church," he told Peter and, quite obviously caring about its continuance, added, "and the gates of hell shall not prevail against it" (Matthew 16:18).

On top of this, Jesus cared about the way the church functioned, particularly the way it helped restore lost sheep, as we mentioned when citing the church-discipline process outlined in Matthew 18:15-20. And take note that Jesus was not just concerned here with the *invisible* church—true believers spread across the globe—but with tangible, local expressions of the church that could even enact discipline over wayward members. In other words, Jesus affirmed the value of the *institutional* church.

THE PURPOSE OF THE CHURCH

Much of the problem with Gulley's account of the church is that he views it as having a purely *horizontal* purpose—that is, how humans relate to humans. The church should be about helping people in need: "feeding the hungry, befriending the lonely, loving the enemy, healing the sick."[28]

While these things are certainly within the church's overall purview, entirely missing from Gulley's account is any *vertical* purpose for the church (how humans relate to God). No mention is made of the church's call to worship and glorify Jesus. No mention is made of the church being the setting in which God speaks to his people through his word. No mention is made of what God does through the sacraments.

This goes a long way toward explaining why Gulley is so frustrated with the church. He sees the main job of the church as solving society's social ills. And he seems upset that it is not doing enough.

Such an approach fits remarkably well with progressive Christianity. If one's religious system is pure moralism, then of course the only applicable categories are the horizontal. The "church" then becomes just another version of the United Way or the local YMCA.

In contrast, the biblical view of the church does not choose between the vertical and horizontal dimensions. It affirms both. Of course, the church is to be a light and blessing to the world. But it is also designed to bring glory and praise to God and to proclaim his truth.

WRONG PROBLEM, WRONG SOLUTION

Gulley rightly points out that the church is an imperfect institution. Indeed, it can be frustrating to watch churches bogged down in their bureaucracy and procedure, failing to do what they are called to do. But Gulley's supposed solution is no solution at all. Rather than jettisoning the institutional church as a man-made creation, as he would have us do, we must return the church to its proper place, an institution ordained and built by Christ himself for his own glory.

We dare not make the church into just another tool to address social ills. Again, while there is certainly a place for the church to serve the community, we cannot forget that the primary task of the church is to worship Christ and proclaim his word.

And let us recall that one day the church *will* be perfect: "'Come, I will show you the Bride, the wife of the Lamb.' And he carried me away in the Spirit to a great, high mountain, and showed me the holy city Jerusalem coming down out of heaven from God, having the glory of God" (Revelation 21:9–11).

CHAPTER 8

Peacemaking Is More Important Than Power

For those frustrated with institutional religion, it can seem as though church leaders are chiefly concerned with having and maintaining their own power. Indeed, it might even seem like churches *attract* power-hungry people, eager to lord it over others. The eighth commandment of progressive Christianity is designed to push back against this problem: *Peacemaking is more important than power.*

We can begin by acknowledging that much in this eighth commandment is right. God does not call church leaders to heavy-handed self-preservation, but to humble, sacrificial service. As Peter charges elders, "Shepherd the flock of God... not domineering over those in your charge, but being examples to the flock" (1 Peter 5:2–3).

Gulley makes his case by providing several examples of bad church leadership—pastors/elders hungry for control and willing to step on (and over) others to get it. I am sure most Christians could tell similar stories from their own experience. However, as in prior chapters, Gulley sometimes has the right diagnosis but the wrong (or woefully incomplete) cure. As we shall see below, in order to rid the church of bad authority, Gulley offers an overly egalitarian approach to leadership that may end up stripping the church of the authority it really does need.

AUTHORITY VS. AUTHORITARIANISM

Gulley makes a proper distinction between authority and authoritarianism. While the former is legitimate, the latter is destructive. Authoritarianism is a heavy-handed, top-down, near-abusive form of leadership that can harm individuals and the church as a whole. Jesus himself recognized the dangers of authoritarian leadership: "You know that the rulers of the Gentiles lord it over them, and their great ones exercise authority over them. It shall not be so among you. But whoever would be great among you must be your servant" (Matthew 20:25–26). Gulley is also right to suggest that authoritarian leadership should be dealt with sooner rather than later: "The sooner authoritarianism is challenged, the healthier the church will be."[29]

But the question immediately arises: how does one know if leadership is authoritarian? Gulley offers a helpful consideration: "Does it build others up or does it put them down?"[30] This echoes the words of Paul: "For even if I boast a little too much of our authority, which the Lord gave for building you up and not for destroying you" (2 Corinthians 10:8).

As we shall see, however, much depends on how one understands the difference between building up and putting down.

WHAT DOES LEGITIMATE AUTHORITY LOOK LIKE?

While Gulley is to be commended for calling out authoritarian leadership, some questions remain about what the exercise of good authority looks like. What is the extent of the church's legitimate authority?

This is where things become a little fuzzy. For example, we might wonder whether the church (or its leaders) have the authority to condemn false doctrine. Can church leaders use their authority to uphold truth and reject error?

Apparently, Gulley doesn't think so. He tells the story of a female pastor who was examined by a committee over concerns regarding her progressive theology. But in Gulley's mind the questioning was itself an abuse of power: "[The committee] had moved from having genuine authority to wielding authoritarian authority, from building others up to tearing others down." The committee, says Gulley, was just about "command and control."[31]

How is upholding sound doctrine an abuse of authority? Does the church have no control over what is taught? Doesn't Paul tell Titus that it is an elder's job "to give instruction in sound doctrine and also to rebuke those who contradict it" (Titus 1:9)? And don't all authorities, even legitimate godly ones, still need *some* level of "command and control"? If they don't, are they really authorities?

Such confusion and inconsistency raises questions about Gulley's view of church authority. It almost seems like *any* exercise of authority is viewed as inappropriate, tyrannical, or somewhere in between. And such sentiments are not unusual within progressive Christianity. As we've seen in earlier chapters, the progressive package, at its core, has a distinct anti-authority vibe. No one can tell us what to do or what to believe (although, ironically, Gulley's entire book is about what to do and what to believe)!

WHAT DOES IT MEAN TO PURSUE PEACE?

If people in the church should pursue peace instead of power, as Gulley suggests, then what exactly does that mean? Incredibly, he takes the opportunity to make his case for pacifism and to chide the American church for supporting the military. So "peace," according to Gulley, is once again viewed in purely *horizontal* terms. It is peace among nations. It is lack of military conflict.

Leaving the issue of pacifism aside (there's no space to address it here), we can certainly agree that bringing reconciliation to broken human relationships is a fundamental biblical value. As already observed, the Bible speaks of forgiving one another (Luke 17:4), being reconciled to one another (Matthew 5:24; Acts 7:26), husbands and wives reconciling (1 Corinthians 7:11), and the removal of hostility between groups (Ephesians 2:16).

However, missing entirely from Gulley's analysis is any consideration of *how* this horizontal peace is achieved. Do we simply try harder? Does the church become a miniature version of the UN? Do we protest the various wars and armed conflicts around the world?

The Scriptures provide an answer to the question of how peace is achieved: "For he [Jesus] himself is our peace, who has made us both one and has broken down in his flesh the dividing wall of hostility" (Ephesians 2:14). The power to love one another and to keep the bond of peace begins with understanding God's love for us in Christ. The latter is the foundation for the former. "We love because he first loved us" (1 John 4:19).

In other words, *horizontal* peace (between man and man) begins first with recognizing our need for *vertical* peace (between God and man). And only Jesus can provide such vertical peace with God.

Remarkably, Gulley seems uninterested in how Jesus brings peace. For him, peace is purely a political and social concept. Again, progressive Christianity, with its disinterest in doctrine—and therefore its disinterest in Jesus—is reduced to mere moralism.

RIGHT PROBLEM, WRONG SOLUTION

Gulley is right to point out the problems with authoritarian church leaders who seek to rule over the flock rather than gently shepherd it. Such leaders can do serious damage to individual members and to the church as a whole. But while Gulley is correct on the diagnosis, doubts remain about the cure. In an effort to rid the church of authoritarian leaders, as he understands them, he may have to rid the church of authority altogether. Ironically, that makes the church even more vulnerable to abusive individuals and false teachings.

Bad leadership is not solved by having no leadership. Instead, bad leadership is to be replaced with godly, gentle, Christ-centered leadership.

Moreover, Gulley continues to think only in horizontal terms. Without Jesus and without the good news of the gospel, he never explains how the arduous and near-impossible task of peacekeeping is to be achieved. Apparently, local churches should just try harder and do more.

That kind of peacekeeping becomes a moralistic yoke around our necks—a plow we must pull in our own strength. We would do better to turn to Jesus, the one who is the great bringer of peace. And he gives it freely: "Peace I leave with you; my peace I give to you" (John 14:27).

CHAPTER 9

We Should Care More about Love and Less about Sex

As we've already observed, progressive Christianity is decidedly moralistic: what matters is not what you believe, but how you behave. How curious, then, that this approach is absent when it comes to issues regarding sex. When sex is in view, suddenly progressives are for moral freedom and moral choice. Such an approach is evident in the ninth commandment: *We should care more about love and less about sex.*

From a rhetorical perspective, such language is quite effective. After all, it tells people what they already want to hear—you have all the sexual freedom you desire and, at the same time, you're a good person who is all about "love." It's a complete win-win. You can maintain any questionable sexual activity even as you congratulate yourself on your moral superiority.

Gulley's book expands this cliché into a full-blown argument for sexual freedom. And he does so by adopting an all-too-common strategy. Let's walk through it.

STEP 1: TOUT THE MORAL VIRTUES OF THOSE IN SEXUAL SIN

The first step in the playbook is to show that people engaging in the disputed sexual behavior are genuinely nice, wonderful, and all-around virtuous folks. This move is designed to make people second-guess whether the sexual sin is all that bad. After all, if it's so bad, how could such wonderful people be doing it? Put another way, if wonderful people engage in a behavior that I think is wrong, then maybe I ought to rethink whether that behavior is really wrong after all.

Gulley executes this move brilliantly. His first example is of a couple in their eighties who are living and sleeping together outside of marriage. He tells us they are "kind," they "warmly welcome" people into their "modest home," and that pictures of "grandchildren lined the walls."[32]

Here we glimpse how Gulley's strategy is largely built on the premise that something is wrong only if the people doing it are unpleasant. In fact, he draws this conclusion directly: "The home they created was one of deep love and mutual respect... nothing about any of that *felt* like sin to me."[33]

But this is not the way Christians think about morality. Christians don't claim something is only wrong when it's done by unpleasant people. And we don't judge a behavior based on how the surrounding circumstances may "feel" to us. We argue that something is bad if it *conflicts with God's character*, which is reflected in his moral commandments.

Thus, Christians would argue that it is very possible—in fact, very common—for very nice people with many other virtues to be engaged in behavior that is very wrong. It's not just serial-killer-types who commit sins. Even the sweet old lady next door can commit sins, even big ones.

Of course, Gulley (and postmodern people in general) do not live out their premise consistently. If being nice makes a behavior okay, then what happens when a very nice person turns out to be engaged in something they find reprehensible? Molesting children, for example. They certainly wouldn't argue, in such an instance, that we must accept such behavior.

STEP 2: INSIST THAT GOD HAS BIGGER THINGS TO WORRY ABOUT

The next step in the strategy is to downplay God's holiness. He's not concerned about sexual sin anyway. It doesn't really bother him; he has more pressing concerns. Gulley states this plainly to the elderly couple, "You know, friends, I think God has bigger things to worry about. Let's just be grateful you have each other."[34]

One is certainly free to portray God in this manner. Indeed, progressives often portray God as a laid-back sort of fellow—a cuddly grandfather figure who doesn't want to intrude into your life, but just wants you to be happy. Yet this is not the God of the Bible. The God of the Bible is infinitely holy and actually talks a good bit about sexual activity and sexual sin. And that's not just because God is prudish and old-school, but because sexual sin hits at the heart of our humanity, viciously assaulting marriage because it is intended to uniquely reflect the union of Christ and his church (Ephesians 5:32).

STEP 3: SHOW THAT THE DISPUTED SEXUAL BEHAVIOR LEADS TO GOOD RESULTS

This third strategic step is similarly brilliant. For at this point, Gulley shows how the sexual sin brings some positive outcome, or at least how the sexual activity helps ameliorate other problems.

Lurking behind this argument is an unspoken premise, namely that something *is* good—indeed, *must be* good—if it *leads to* something good. That is, a good outcome serves as proof-positive of the moral value of the behavior that produced it. In terms of the elderly couple, Gulley notes that they were financially strapped, so living together (as a couple) enabled them to make ends meet. Also, they were "lonely" and needed the companionship.[35]

This strategy works well, of course, because anyone who then insists the couple should not be living together in this way sounds like they are callous to the couple's financial situation and care nothing for their loneliness. Once more, however, this is not the biblical perspective. One can still be very compassionate and sympathetic about their situation, while also reminding them they need to follow God's guidance for sexual activity. The two are not mutually exclusive.

Moreover, Christians should challenge the underlying idea that difficult circumstances justify sinful behavior. An inability to pay my rent does not give me the right to rob a bank, and I'm sure the postmodern folks would agree with that. Yet that is essentially the logic they use to try to whitewash sexual sin.

STEP 4: PORTRAY THOSE WHO ARE AGAINST CERTAIN SEXUAL BEHAVIORS AS MEAN-SPIRITED AND CRUEL

Every good story has a foil, a nemesis you can cheer against. In this story of the elderly couple, Gulley describes the church elder who first informed him of this couple's situation. Instead of the warm, positive description given to the elderly couple, this man gets the opposite.

He is portrayed as "critical," "unduly upset," one who "roundly condemned" others and was eager to enforce his "rather extensive sexual code."[36] Gulley even implies he is financially stingy and unwilling to help this elderly couple. According to Gulley's overly simplistic portrayal, it's not the people engaging in sexual sin who are the problem. It is the guy who points it out!

This is the backward morality of postmodernity (however inconsistently applied). In those categories where it's found to serve the larger progressive agenda (e.g., bank robbery, no; sexual sin, yes), the criteria for weighing good and bad are reversed.

Completely missing from Gulley's account, however, is the idea that *sin harms people* and that perhaps this elder was genuinely concerned with the damage that sexual sin causes in peoples' lives. In other words, is it possible—a shocking idea to many in our postmodern world—that it is actually *loving* to confront sin?

STEP 5: INSIST JESUS IS ON YOUR SIDE

The final step in the justification of sexual sin is ostensibly to enlist the help of Jesus. To do so, Gulley trots out the standard clichés about Jesus being more gracious to sinners than to legalists. He even appeals (not surprisingly) to the story of Jesus being anointed by the sinful woman.[37]

What Gulley leaves out, however, is that the woman came to Jesus not defiant in her sins but repentant of them! Indeed, Jesus indicates that "her sins... are many" but that they "are forgiven" (Luke 7:47). Yes, Jesus forgives sinners. But we must acknowledge and admit we *are* sinners.

In sum, Gulley's ninth commandment is a masterpiece of progressive Christianity. It runs through the classic playbook of justifying sexual sin and, at first glance, can seem quite compelling. But ultimately it just doesn't hold up. We are not called to care about love instead of sex. We are called to care about both. As Paul reminds us, "Set the believers an example in speech, in conduct, in love, in faith, in purity" (1 Timothy 4:12).

CHAPTER 10

Life in This World Is More Important Than the Afterlife

We come, finally, to the tenth and last "commandment" of progressive Christianity. This one is truly a classic: *Life in this world is more important than the afterlife.*

It's hard to imagine a single statement that better captures the ethos of progressive Christianity than this one. Indeed, this tenth commandment reveals the profound pivot that progressive folks have taken, actively turning away from matters eternal to focus on matters earthly. Let's not worry ourselves about what happens after death, we are told, because no one really knows anyway. All that matters is helping the poor, feeding the hungry, and relieving human suffering.

This commandment marks a fitting end to this short volume because it so concisely embodies many of the values of liberal Christianity pointed out by Machen so many years ago. Here are a few of them, echoing some of the most salient points from previous chapters.

PRIORITIZING THE HORIZONTAL OVER THE VERTICAL

For progressive Christians, humans have a real problem. But it's not that they are rebellious sinners who have offended a holy God. Rather, the problem for humanity is that there is suffering, war, poverty, and disease.

In other words, human problems are defined by progressives in purely *horizontal* terms (the way humans relate to the world or to fellow humans), and not in *vertical* terms (the way man relates to God). As a result, the highest ideal of progressive Christianity can be nothing other than fixing present, temporal problems. Speaking of eternity is seen as a distraction at best, and a waste of time at worst. In fact, Gulley laments the church's "preoccupation" with and "overemphasis" on the afterlife and how "fortunes are spent saving people from the imaginary dangers of imaginary places."[38]

PREACHING MORALISM NOT SALVATION

If there's no eternity to worry about, then what should humans focus on? Doing good works, of course. Helping our fellow man. The hallmark of progressive Christianity is a deep commitment to being "good" and doing "good" things. Gulley states, "If the Church were Christian, we would do what Jesus did—equip one another to live better in this world and stop fretting about the next one."[39]

Of course, anyone familiar with the teachings of Jesus should find this statement genuinely stunning. Jesus was quite concerned with the next world and spoke of it often. Consider just one example: "Do not fear those who kill the body but cannot kill the soul. Rather fear him who can destroy both soul and body in hell" (Matthew 10:28).

If there is no hell, no sin, and no judgment, then progressive Christianity has no other option than to become a moralistic religion.

CLAIMING UNCERTAINTY WHILE ESPOUSING CERTAINTY

At the core of Gulley's argument is the belief that hell isn't real. "I decided not to invest any effort in saving people's souls from a hell I didn't believe in."[40] Indeed, throughout that same chapter Gulley repeatedly states that there is no hell. He is banking his eternal fate (as well as the fate of others) on this conviction.

But how does he *know* this? Missing from Gulley's argument is any reason to think he could know such a thing. He just states his claim without any basis to back it up.

The irony of such a claim is that Gulley actually positions himself as the humble seeker, uncertain of his beliefs. "I've not yet arrived at a definitive understanding of God and I don't suspect I ever will."[41]

This highlights one of the most notable and pernicious techniques of progressive Christianity: claim uncertainty on the front end, but then slip your own certain convictions into the picture later, hoping no one will notice the essential hypocrisy and incoherence of such a position.

CONCLUSION

So we see that Gulley's final commandment masterfully encapsulates three hallmarks of progressive Christianity. It focuses on man instead of God, downplays doctrine for morality, and claims uncertainty while all the while being very, very certain of itself.

Tragically, the progressive position clouds the real message of Christianity—the real message of Jesus. Jesus cared about the suffering of humans, and he has called Christians to do the same. We do not, however, address human suffering as an act of moralism, but as a response to the grace shown to us at the cross.

Moreover, we don't address temporal human suffering exclusively. For even if we could somehow alleviate *all* human suffering, it would do exactly nothing to meet humanity's greatest need. As Jesus reminds us, "What will it profit a man if he gains the whole world and forfeits his soul?" (Matthew 16:26).

ENDNOTES

1   J. Gresham Machen, *Christianity and Liberalism* (Grand Rapids, MI: Eerdmans, 2009)

2   Philip Gulley, *If the Church Were Christian: Rediscovering the Values of Jesus* (San Francisco, CA: HarperOne, 2010)

3   https://cac.org/returning-to-essentials-2017-11-30/

4   Gulley, 16, 17

5   Machen, 96

6   Michael F. Bird, *Jesus the Eternal Son: Answering Adoptionist Christology* (Grand Rapids, MI: Eerdmans, 2017)

7   C.S. Lewis, *Mere Christianity,* Revised & Enlarged edition (San Francisco, CA: HarperOne, 2105), 55–56

8   For more on the latter, see Larry Hurtado, *One God One Lord: Early Christian Devotion and Ancient Christian Monotheism,* 2nd Reissue edition (London: T&T Clark, 2000)

9   Machen, 47

10   Ibid, 64

11   However progressives may define or understand "brokenness" on the personal level, evangelicals will rightly recognize that all brokenness, by any definition, is an outgrowth of the fall—a fallen, broken world and a fallen, broken humanity in which all are sinners.

12 Gulley, 40, 30

13 Ibid, 33

14 Ibid, 37–40

15 Ibid, 44, 43

16 Ibid, 44, emphasis mine

17 Ibid, 54, 57, 61

18 Ibid, 67

19 Ibid

20 Machen, 47–48

21 Gulley, 93

22 Ibid, 116, 118

23 To be clear, Christians don't believe everything in the Bible is equally clear—some things are difficult to understand. But they do believe that "those things which are necessary for salvation" (WCF 1.7) are clear.

24 Dan Kimball, *They Like Jesus but Not the Church: Insights from Emerging Generations* (Grand Rapids, MI: Zondervan, 2007)

25 Gulley, 123

26 Ibid, 125

27 Ibid, 137

28 Ibid, 126

29 Ibid, 146

30 Ibid, 144

31 Ibid, 145

32 Ibid, 157–159

33 Ibid, 160

34 Ibid, 158

35 Ibid

36 Ibid, 159

37 Ibid, 166

38 Ibid, 175, 176, 184

39 Ibid, Gulley 184

40 Ibid, Gulley 181

41 Ibid, 18

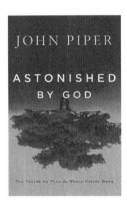

Astonished by God
Ten Truths to Turn the World Upside Down

John Piper | 192 pages

Turn your world on its head.

bit.ly/AstonishedbyGod

The Most Encouraging Book on Hell Ever

Thor Ramsey | 97 pages

The biblical view of hell is under attack. But if hell freezes over, we lose a God of love and holiness, the good new of Jesus Christ, and so much more.

bit.ly/HELLBOOK

Do Ask, Do Tell, Let's Talk
Why and How Christians Should Have Gay Friends

Brad Hambrick | 118 pages

Conversations among friends accomplish more than debates between opponents.

bit.ly/DoAsk

Can I Smoke Pot?
Marijuana in Light of Scripture

Tom Breeden and
Mark L. Ward, Jr. | 101 pages

Pot is legal in more and more places. And
Christians are allowed to drink alcohol, right?
So really... what's the issue?

bit.ly/POTBOOK

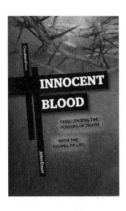

Innocent Blood
Challenging the Powers of Death with the Gospel of Life

John Ensor | 108 pages

Explore the striking relationships between the
scandal of the gospel and the tragedy of abortion.

bit.ly/THEBLOOD

"But God..."
The Two Words at the Heart of the Gospel

Casey Lute | 100 pages

Just two words.
Understand their use in Scripture, and you
will never be the same.

bit.ly/ButGOD

Smooth Stones
Bringing Down the Giant Questions of Apologetics

Joe Coffey | 101 pages

Street-level apologetics for everyday Christians.

Because faith in Jesus makes sense. And you don't need an advanced degree to understand why.

bit.ly/CPStones

The Joy Project:
An Introduction to Calvinism (with Study Guide)

Tony Reinke | 168 pages

True happiness isn't found. It finds you.

bit.ly/JOYPROJECT

Who Am I?
Identity in Christ

Jerry Bridges | 91 pages

Jerry Bridges unpacks Scripture to give the Christian eight clear, simple, interlocking answers to one of the most essential questions of life.

bit.ly/WHOAMI

Made in the USA
Las Vegas, NV
06 April 2021

20935884R00033